# GUIDE

## by MEGAN WRIGHT

## getting started

Getting started with essential oils and living a more natural lifestyle? This easy guide walks you through the basics of Young Living® and ways to incorporate our favorite essential oils and clean products into your daily life.

*Disclosure: We are not medical professionals and the information in this guide is not intended to diagnose, treat, cure, or prevent any disease. We are specifically recommending Young Living essential oils. You are responsible for your own health journey.*

Copyright © 2021 by Megan Wright Design Co.
Design & photography by Megan Wright Design Co.
Published by Growing Healthy Homes
meganwrightdesign.com
Young Living Brand Partner

## This guide belongs to

_____

### member *info*

*This is the information you're going to want to hang on to forever. Write it down and save it for future orders.*

Member ID _____ PIN _____

Login/Username _____

Password _____

### how to *order again*
Visit youngliving.com and click Sign In
Enter username + password
Search product and Add to Cart or
Add to Subscription (the best way to order)

### customer service
1-800-371-3515 or customerservice@youngliving.com
LIVE CHAT available

## Chapter 01 / getting started

Member info .................................................................................3
Welcome ......................................................................................6
Essential oil basics ......................................................................8
Why Young Living®? ...................................................................9
Ways to use essential oils ........................................................10
Where to apply oils ..................................................................11
Favorite everyday oils quick guide .........................................12

## Chapter 02 / targeted support

Staying well / immune support ..............................................16
Respiratory needs ...................................................................20
Muscles, joints & tension ........................................................22
Digestion & gut health ............................................................24
Energy & NingXia® Red ...........................................................26

## Chapter 03 / clean home

Gatekeepers .............................................................................30
Thieves® Line ...........................................................................32
Thieves Cleaner .......................................................................34
Laundry ....................................................................................36
Clean home recipes ................................................................38
Diffuser Blends .......................................................................40

## Chapter 04 / oily life

Glowy skin ................................................................................48
Oily routines for her ................................................................50
Oily routines for him ...............................................................52
Clean bathroom simple swaps ...............................................54
Oily routines for littles ............................................................56
Oils & emotions .......................................................................62
Bedtime routines .....................................................................65

## Chapter 05 / oily details

Ordering / Subscribe to Save ..................................................68
Safety tips ................................................................................70
Sharing the Oily Life ................................................................72
Recipe journal .........................................................................75
Roller blend quick guide .........................................................88
Summer staples ......................................................................89
Oily wishlist .............................................................................90
Simple swaps ..........................................................................93
Targeted Support quick list ....................................................94

# welcome
*to the oily life*

We are thrilled that you've decided to join us on this wellness journey. We think you made the best decision to support your overall health and live a more joyful life. One of our favorite things about oils is how easy it is to fit them into our lives. From morning until night, they're there to support our physical and emotional needs in the most simple, beautiful ways.

This book is your guide to help you get started. We encourage you to begin with the area you want to focus on the most and take the first step. When you're ready, take the next step. Each step will add up over time for a life of wellness.

## OUR COMMUNITY

We know learning about oils can be a little intimidating at first. Trust us—we had a lot of questions when we got started! That's why we wrote this book. We want you to know that you're not alone. You're a part of a growing and thriving community full of support, education, and encouragement. Our team offers classes, webinars, and private online support groups to help you learn about all of our favorite products.

If you choose to pursue Young Living as a Brand Partner, we also have exclusive tools to help you learn about making a little (or a lot) of extra income. Interested in learning about becoming a Brand Partner? Head on over to page 72 for all the details and ask your enroller to get you plugged in.

### FAVORITE RESOURCES & ONLINE SUPPORT GROUPS
*plug in here for education and support*

_____

_____

_____

_____

CHAPTER
# 01

*let's get started*
# the basics

## WHAT IS AN ESSENTIAL OIL?

An essential oil is the essence of a plant. It gives the plant its unique scent. When carefully extracted from trees, flowers, herbs, rinds of fruit, and other parts of a plant, it provides therapeutic benefits. Essential oils have been used since ancient times for medicinal reasons, beauty, spiritual support, and more. They are super concentrated, so a little goes a long way.

### how fast do oils work?

Within 22 seconds, molecules reach the brain
Within 2 minutes, found in bloodstream
Within 20 minutes, every cell has been affected

## ESSENTIAL OILS ARE PRETTY AMAZING
*They go so far beyond making your home smell pretty*

*a few things oils can do*

**01/** Can support the body at a cellular level. They help to maintain homeostasis and keep us well.

**02/** A natural tool to help our body do what it was created to do.

**03/** Can help with balance, sleep, immunity, stress, happy bellies, healthy breathing, hormones, aches, focus, the list goes on...

**04/** Can replace the toxic cleaners, candles, and harsh personal care products in your home.

*why young living?*

## THE BEST
*essential oils in the world*

Essential oils have become trendy and you probably spot them on store shelves, but they're not new. Young Living® started small in 1993 and has pioneered the modern-day essential oil movement. Young Living inspires wellness, purpose, and abundance by distilling nature's greatest gifts into pure essential oils. With a commitment to plant purity and essential oil potency, Young Living continues to grow, inspiring millions to transform their lives.

# quality matters
*the seed to seal promise*

It's important to understand the differences in quality when purchasing essential oils. You can find many low-quality essential oils at the store that are typically "fragrance-grade" and filled with synthetic chemicals, adulterated and unethically sourced, all while being labeled "pure." Yuck! You don't want to breathe that in and you *definitely* don't want to put that on your skin.

We trust Young Living because they have a Seed to Seal® standard. Young Living manages every step—from the seed planted at the farm all the way through distillation and bottling. Each batch is tested multiple times and, if it doesn't reach their high standards, it's tossed out. Young Living is the only company to own and partner with farms all over the world (you can even visit the farms!) Young Living values transparency, quality, and sustainability You can visit *seedtoseal.com* to learn more.

*sourcing. science. standards*

# *ways to use* essential oils

Essential oils are so versatile. We use them for pretty much everything.
These are a few ways we recommend using Young Living Essential Oils®.

### 01
### DIFFUSE
*- aromatic use -*

### 02
### APPLY *to* SKIN
*- topical use -*

### 03
### INGEST
*- internal use -*

Diffusing oils can help us experience less stress, more relaxation, better focus, a mood boost, deeper sleep, improved air quality, and that "clean house" smell (without toxic chemicals from candles and air fresheners).

Essential oils are rapidly absorbed into your bloodstream when applied topically to the skin and are very effective at creating balance and helping your body do what it's meant to do.

Young Living oils are the best of the best. Because of this, we can safely ingest Vitality™ oils (bottles with the white labels) and use them to support our health in a targeted way.

## *get oiling checklist*

### AROMATIC

☐ Add 6-10 drops of oil to your diffuser

☐ Add a drop to the palms of your hands and inhale

☐ Add oils to diffuser jewelry

☐ Inhale straight out of the bottle

☐ Add a few drops of oil to a cotton ball and drop in your trash can, in your car, or other areas that may be a little smelly.

### TOPICAL

☐ Add essential oils to roller bottles and make your own blends & recipes

☐ Apply to the area of your body that needs support

☐ The bottoms of feet is a great place to start applying oils

☐ Dilute with a carrier oil for hot oils or when applying to little ones

### INTERNAL

☐ Add 1 - 2 drops of citrus oils to your water

☐ Add oils to an empty vegetable capsule and top with coconut or olive oil

☐ Use a drop under your tongue or swipe inside of your cheek for quick absorbtion

☐ Flavor your favorite foods with oils

# quick guide to our favorite oils

### A CHEAT SHEET TO OUR TOP 24 OILS

# where to apply essential oils

Bottoms of feet *(especially for little ones)*
Wrists            Along spine
Chest             Temples
Stomach           Crown of head
Behind ears       Back of neck

Look into Vita-Flex points as well. Apply where you need support. Avoid eyes, inside of ears, and sensitive areas. Always test by applying to the forearm first and follow directions on the label.

## WHAT IS A CARRIER OIL?

Carrier oils are fatty vegetable oils which are used to dilute the essential oils and help "carry" them into the skin. Diluting the essential oil changes the concentration of the essential oil, but not the awesome benefits. Carrier oils are very important to use when applying to little ones or using "hot" oils.

### favorite carrier oils

Coconut oil        Grapeseed oil
Jojoba oil         Young Living's V-6
Avocado oil        Olive Oil

## how to mix up your first roller recipe

Grab some 10 ml roller bottles from Amazon or Etsy and some fractionated coconut oil or carrier oil of choice. Add 15 - 30 drops of essential oil to your empty roller and fill the remainder with carrier oil. Now just roll it on. You'll find some go-to recipes here in this guide to help get you started. Easy-peasy.

EVERY DAY FAVORITES
*quick guide*

# thieves® / + Vitality™
+ Wellness keeper
+ Fall & Winter must-have
+ Throat soother
+ Add 1-2 drops to honey tea when feeling unwell

USES: *aromatic | topical | internal*

# lemon / + Vitality™
+ Cleansing
+ Detoxing
+ Mood boosting
+ Sticky residue remover
+ Digestion helper

USES: *aromatic | topical | internal*

# peppermint / + Vitality™
+ Energizing
+ Happy digestion
+ Head tension
+ Concentration
+ Fresh breath

USES: *aromatic | topical | internal*

# peace & calming®
+ Anxious feelings
+ Tantrum tamer
+ Restful sleep
+ Calms nerves
+ Soothes little ones

USES: *aromatic | topical*

# lavender / + Vitality™
+ Skin soother
+ Stress relieving
+ Sweet sleep
+ Springtime woes

USES: *aromatic | topical | internal*

# r.c.™
+ Easy breathing
+ Respiratory
+ Natural chest rub
+ Opens sinuses
+ Invigorating

USES: *aromatic | topical*

# orange / + Vitality™
+ Mood booster
+ Creativity & harmony
+ High in limonene
+ Natural teeth whitener
+ Add to DIY furniture polish

USES: *aromatic | topical | internal*

# frankincense / + Vitality™
+ Grounding for emotions
+ Skin magic
+ Focus, prayer, & meditation
+ Immunity boost

USES: *aromatic | topical | internal*

# EVERY DAY FAVORITES
## quick guide

## valor®
+ Emotional support
+ Bravery & confidence
+ Worry & overwhelm
+ Grounding natural perfume

USES: *aromatic | topical | internal*

## stress away™
+ Combats stress
+ Induces relaxation
+ Bedtime favorite
+ Natural perfume
+ Apply to wrists, chest, or shoulders

USES: *aromatic | topical*

## digize®/ + *Vitality*™
+ Healthy digestion
+ Tummy troubles
+ Gotta-go relief.
+ Take in a capsule when traveling overseas

USES: *topical | internal*

## panaway®
+ Muscles & joints
+ Apply after exercise or sports
+ Soothe neck & back
+ Add to Epsom salt foot soak
+ Dilute and apply to temples & forehead to soothe head

USES: *aromatic | topical*

## raven™
+ Healthy breathing
+ Natural chest rub
+ Opens sinuses
+ A go-to for respiratory needs
+ Use along with Thieves Cough Drops

USES: *aromatic | topical*

## citrus fresh™/
+ *Vitality*™
+ Ditch candles & diffuse
+ "Clean house" scent
+ Odors be gone
+ Add a drop of Citrus Fresh Vitality to water to help curb appetite

USES: *aromatic | topical | internal*

## cedarwood
+ Add to a roller with Vetiver and Lavender for focus support
+ Diffuse with Lavender for sleep
+ Add to shampoo for hair growth
+ Calming

USES: *aromatic | topical*

## melrose
+ Ear support
+ Spot treat blemishes
+ Add to roller with Thieves
+ Apply to skin irritations
+ Can use on funky toenails

USES: *aromatic | topical*

EVERY DAY FAVORITES
*quick guide*

## christmas spirit™
+ Candle dupe/diffuser must-have
+ Cozy and comforting aroma
+ Uplifts mood and boosts wellness
+ Immune & respiratory benefits
USES: *aromatic | topical | internal*

## grapefruit/+ *Vitality*™
+ Add a drop to water
+ A diffuser recipe favorite
+ Uplifting and refreshing
+ Cleansing & metabolism booster
USES: *aromatic | topical | internal*

## copaiba/+ *Vitality*™
+ Rub on teething baby's gums
+ Apply topically with PanAway on muscles or sore areas
+ Supports body while dealing with inflammation
+ Add to throat spray with Thieves
USES: *aromatic | topical | internal*

## lime/+ *Vitality*™
+ A dreamy diffuser must-have
+ Add a drop to water with NingXia Red and Sulfurzyme powder for a healthy drink
+ Uplifting and motivating
USES: *aromatic | topical | internal*

## endoflex™/+ *Vitality*™
+ Thyroid & hormone helper
+ Energy booster
+ Apply over thyroid/adrenals each morning for energy
+ Apply over liver area for kiddos or teens with big emotions
USES: *aromatic | topical | internal*

## oregano/+ *Vitality*™
+ Immune powerhouse
+ Must-have oil for Winter wellness toolbox
+ Add to capsule with Thieves and olive oil when feeling unwell
+ Add to roller with Thieves
USES: *aromatic | topical | internal*

## pine
+ Emotionally grounding
+ Helps when feeling anxious
+ Happy lungs and sinuses
+ Diffuse with Orange at bedtime
+ Add to DIY furniture polish
USES: *aromatic | topical*

## white angelica™
+ Emotional support
+ Favorite for overwhelm & worry
+ Apply to tops of shoulders when dealing with negativity
USES: *aromatic | topical*

CHAPTER
02

# *targeted support*
# staying well

WELLNESS BOOSTERS

STAYING WELL

*targeted support*

# thieves®
*Thieves oil is our health keeper, immunity booster, and a favorite tool to fight the yuck.*

**WAYS TO USE:**
- Apply to feet or spine as a part of your wellness routine.
- Drop Thieves Vitality™ under tongue for immunity boost.
- Dilute and apply daily for fewer missed days of work & school.
- Add a drop of Thieves Vitality to honey and hot water and drink up.
- Soothe your throat with Thieves Vitality in tea.
- Diffuse for clean air, especially in winter months.

**OILS IN THIS BLEND:**
*Clove | Cinnamon + Rosemary + Lemon + Eucalyptus*

---

*recipe*

**WELLNESS ROLLER**

In a 10 ml roller, add essentials oils and top with carrier oil

**OILS:**

+ 15 drops Thieves         + 7 drops Melrose
+ 15 drops Frankincense    + 7 drops Oregano
+ 15 drops Lemon           + carrier oil of choice

**TO USE:** *roll on bottoms of feet or along spine as often as needed when fighting off the yuck.*

---

*morning wellness routine*

**01/** Start the day right by drinking a packet of NingXia Red®. This will energize your day and support total body wellness.

**02/** Add 1 - 2 drops of Lemon Vitality to your water (glass or stainless steel cup) to help rid your body of toxins.

**03/** Apply Thieves to the bottom of your feet each day as a part of your wellness routine. Diffuse Thieves to purify the air.

**04/** Bust out Raven for happy airways when needed. Diffuse or dilute and apply topically to the chest and neck to breathe deeply.

**TARGETED SUPPORT:** *staying well*

**THIEVES TEA**
When your throat needs to be soothed or your wellness needs a boost, pour yourself a cup of this.

*thieves tea recipe*

*ingredients*
+ 1 tbsp. organic honey
+ 1 drop Thieves Vitality™
+ 1 drop Lemon Vitality™
+ Green Tea bag
+ add hot water

*recipe*

### THIEVES HONEY THROAT SPRAY

In a 2 oz glass spray bottle, add ingredients & top with distilled water:

INGREDIENTS:
+ 1 oz Thieves Mouthwash
+ 10 drops Thieves Vitality
+ 10 drops Lemon Vitality
+ 10 drops Copaiba Vitality
+ 5 drops Clove Vitality
+ 1 tbsp. raw honey

TO USE: *Give the bottle a shake and spray throat to soothe as often as needed.*

## wellness staples *checklist*

**ESSENTIAL OILS**
- ☐ Oregano
- ☐ Melrose™
- ☐ R.C.™
- ☐ SniffleEase™
- ☐ Breathe Again™

**SUPPLEMENTS**
- ☐ Inner Defense™
- ☐ Thieves Cough® Drops
- ☐ NingXia Red®
- ☐ Super D & Super C™
- ☐ Thieves® Chest Rub

TARGETED SUPPORT: *staying well*

# wellness diffuser blend

We've ditched candles, air fresheners, and toxic room sprays and just diffuse oils now. We love diffusing Thieves® for its powerful health and wellness benefits, especially in the colder months. Plus, it smells like cinnamon-y clove Fall goodness. You won't even miss your candles.

## SPICED ORANGE VANILLA

+ 3 drops Thieves
+ 6 drops Vanilla
+ 6 drops Orange

MORE DIFFUSER BLENDS | *page 40*

## *springtime roller*

In a 10 ml roller, add essentials oils and top with carrier oil

OILS:

+ 15 drops Lavender
+ 15 drops Lemon
+ 15 drops Peppermint

TO USE: *Apply on neck, jaw, over eustachian tube area, or chest as often as needed, especially when pollen count is high.*

## SPRINGTIME WOES

*When everything is blooming or seasons are changing, we love this little trio.*

### *diffuser blend*

3 Lavender + 3 Lemon + 3 Peppermint

TARGETED SUPPORT: *staying well*

*targeted support*

## JUST BREATHE

### raven™
*Our happy sinuses, airways, and deep-in-the-chest soothing oil. Bonus: It smells like a spa!*

**WAYS TO USE:**
- Add a couple drops to the floor of a steamy shower when feeling stuffy.
- Apply to chest and neck for a cooling effect.
- Mix up a chest rub with Raven and coconut oil to breathe deeply.
- Take this oil to the next level by using with Thieves® Cough Drops.
- Diffuse with Thieves when you need to fight the yuck, especially in the Winter months.

**OILS IN THIS BLEND:**
*Ravintsara + Lemon + Wintergreen + Peppermint + Eucalyptus Radiata*

---

*recipe*

### SNIFFLES ROLLER

In a 10 ml roller, add essentials oils and top with carrier oil

**OILS:**

+ 15 drops R.C.™          + 10 drops Lemon
+ 5 drops Peppermint      + carrier oil of choice

**TO USE:** *Roll on chest or bottoms of feet when feeling stuffy.*

---

## winter *must haves*

*In addition to your prized oils, we recommend adding these to your arsenal so you're prepared to fight whatever comes your way, naturally.*

**01  INNER DEFENSE™** *Immune support & healthy respiratory function*
This supplement contains some heavy-hitting oils like Thieves, Oregano, and Thyme. It's a powerhouse when you need extra immune and respiratory love.

*over-the-counter natural alternatives*

**02  THIEVES CHEST RUB** *Cough, cold, & congestion*
This is a 100% natural, plant-based alternative for coughs and congestion. Safe for the whole family, ages 2 and up. No yucky petroleum in this stuff.

**03  THIEVES COUGH DROPS** *Cough, congestion, & sore throats*
These natural cough drops actually WORK and are worth their weight in gold. Infused with Thieves essential oil and menthol, these cough drops have over-the-counter strength but without the nasty fake dyes, artificial flavors, and processed sugars found in most.

TARGETED SUPPORT: *staying well*

*targeted support*

**MUSCLE ROLLER** *recipe*

In a 10 ml roller, add essentials oils and top with carrier oil

OILS:

+ 15 drops PanAway®
+ 15 drops Peppermint
+ 15 drops Valor®

TO USE: Roll on sore neck, muscles, or joints when needed.

*muscles, joints & tension routine*

01/ Use PanAway on muscles and joints after a workout or when you need extra support.

02/ Apply Peppermint on temples, back of neck, or other areas you're holding tension.

03/ Apply Valor to spine to support healthy alignment.

04/ Soothe your body with an Epsom salt bath. A few oils to add to the epsom salts: Lavender, Stress Away, or Valor.

05/ Soak your tired feet in this relieving foot soak. Warm water + a few drops of PanAway on Epsom salts.

MUSCLES & JOINTS

*targeted support*

# panaway® *Muscle & joint favorite.*

WAYS TO USE:
- Great to soothe muscles before and after exercise.
- Add several drops to an Epsom salt foot soak.
- Apply topically to joints, fingers, and hands to loosen.
- Add several drops to V-6 Vegetable Oil for a massage.
- Add a couple drops of PanAway and Peppermint to a dollop of coconut oil and massage into neck, back, or sore areas.

OILS IN THIS BLEND:
*Wintergreen + Helichrysum + Clove + Peppermint*

**01** DEEP RELIEF™ ROLL-ON
An easy on-the-go roll-on to throw in your purse. It has that refreshing, cooling sensation that feels amazing on a tense neck and shoulders.

**02** CBD MUSCLE RUB
The power of CBD combined with essential oils for amazing relief.

**03** AGILEASE®
Our favorite supplement for healthy joints. Athletes love this, as well as elderly people who may experience a natural, acute inflammation response in joints after exercise.

## oils *checklist*

- PanAway
- Copaiba
- Deep Relief Roll-On
- CBD Muscle Rub

## *supplements*

- AgilEase®
- Golden Turmeric
- AminoWise™
- Sulfurzyme®

*If you're wanting some extra support for your body's natural response to inflammation, joint health, etc., we couldn't recommend looking into these supplements enough. Game changers.*

*targeted support*

## let's chat
# gut health

Gut health plays a huge role in the different functions of the body and our overall well-being. It not only affects our digestion, but can impact our immunity, skin, mood, hormones, energy, sleep—you name it! We often call the gut our second brain. Did you know that issues like depression, anxiety, insomnia, fatigue, and brain fog can all be caused by a gut imbalance?

### digestive wellness tips

We want to make sure everything is moving properly and we're avoiding constipation. Eat real, whole foods and limit sugar and processed foods. Avoid antibiotics as much as possible and consider adding a high quality probiotic to your regimen (like Life 9®) to boost that GOOD gut bacteria. Drink lots of filtered water and use your amazing oils like DiGize™, Peppermint, and Lemon.

*simple steps for happy bellies*

01/ Put a drop of Lemon Vitality™ in your water every day for gentle cleansing effects.

02/ Apply DiGize topically over stomach or swab DiGize Vitality on the inside of cheek when needed.

03/ Put a drop of Peppermint Vitality under tongue after a spicy meal. Inhale when stomach is feeling uneasy.

04/ Take a quality probiotic. Life 9 for adults, Mighty Pro™ for kids.

TARGETED SUPPORT: *digestion*

# digize ™ *Healthy Digestion. Happy Bellies. Healthy Elimination.*

**WAYS TO USE:**
- Swab a drop of DiGize Vitality™ on the inside of cheek after a large meal.
- Apply topically on abdomen for happy tummies.
- Add DiGize Vitality to capsule and take internally when traveling abroad or eating different foods.

**OILS IN THIS BLEND:**
*Tarragon + Ginger +Peppermint + Juniper +Fennel + Lemongrass + Anise + Patchouli*

# peppermint *Perk up & Focus. Happy digestive system.*

**WAYS TO USE:**
- Inhale when stomach is feeling uneasy or driving on winding roads.
- Add a drop of Peppermint Vitality to water after a spicy meal.
- Rub a drop on temples for head tension.
- Diffuse to get you going for the day.
- Add a couple drops of Peppermint Vitality to brownie batter for a yummy mint-chocolate flavor.

---

**TUMMY ROLLER**
In a 10 ml roller, add essentials oils and top with carrier oil
**OILS:**
+ 10 DiGize
+ 10 Peppermint
**TO USE:** *Roll around belly button for upset tummies and healthy elimination*

---

# digestion *favorites*

**PROBIOTIC** *Life 9®*
Probiotic with 17 billion live cultures to help promote healthy digestion and maintain normal intestinal function for the overall support of a healthy immune system.

**KID'S PROBIOTIC** *Kidscents Mighty Pro™*
This probiotic is a kid favorite that tastes like a pixie stick! Add this to your child's nightly routine to support healthy digestion and boost immune system.

**ALKALIME®**
Add to water to enjoy an effervescent drink that helps to naturally support pH balance and soothe the occasional upset stomach or that burning feeling in the chest.

TARGETED SUPPORT: *staying well*

# but first, ningxia
*energy wellness*
*our morning shot of wellness*

Meet our favorite antioxidant drink and game changer in a bottle. NingXia Red® is a tasty powerhouse drink that's jam packed with superfoods to support overall wellness. It contains the wolfberry fruit from NingXia, China which is known for its amazing health perks. Just 2 ounces a day will do a body so good! Get it down the hatch in the morning for steady energy throughout the day.

## WHAT'S IN NINGXIA RED?

*A whole-food supplement made from wolfberry puree, as well as a super blend of blueberry, aronia, cherry, pomegranate, and plum juices. Infused with a blend of Orange, Yuzu, Lemon, and Tangerine essential oils.*

## THE LOWDOWN
*on antioxidants*

Antioxidants protect our bodies and help fight free radicals. Free radicals are harmful molecules that can damage our cells. Let's get all the extra help we can get. Wolfberries are one of the highest known sources of antioxidants and are a natural source of essential vitamins and minerals like zinc, magnesium, calcium, Vitamin B and more. You'll want this goodness daily.

## ningxia red perks

01/ Packed full of antioxidants, amino acids, fiber, and fatty acids. Designed to energize, fortify, and revitalize your body and mind.

02/ The NingXia wolfberry is a rich vegetarian source of zinc, a mineral critical for healthy immunity.

03/ Helps protect against oxidative stress and supports normal cellular function and overall wellness.

04/ Promotes healthy energy levels without caffeine.

05/ Supports healthy digestion and normal eye health.

# targeted support

### THE RED DRINK *recipe*

Drink your Ningxia chilled and straight from the pouch, or mix up our favorite Red Drink for an afternoon treat.

+ 2 oz Ningxia Red®  + 1 drop Lime Vitality™ oil
+ 1 tsp Sulfurzyme® Powder  + filtered water

*In a glass or stainless steel cup, add ice and ingredients. Fill the rest up with filtered water. Grab a glass or stainless steel straw and drink up, buttercup.*

## sulfurzyme
*spotlight*

If you have skin, hair, nails, or joints (and we hope you do), you're likely not getting enough of the compound MSM found in Sulfurzyme. Weak and brittle nails, hair that doesn't grow or isn't healthy, joints that are painful, and skin issues can all be giant billboard signs telling you that you need more nutrition in this area. Skin that's ultra sensitive to the topical use of oils can be another telltale sign. This one supplement can do so much to help you benefit from everything else you're doing with your oils to increase your health.

TARGETED SUPPORT : *energy & total body wellness*

# *drink* recipes

**01 give it to me straight**
2 oz chilled NingXia Red® in a shot glass or pouch

**02 mama mocktail**
2 oz NingXia Red + 1 drop Lime Vitality™ in your fav sparkling water over ice

**03 dreamsicle shot**
2 oz NingXia Red + a drop of Orange Vitality in a shot glass

**04 pick-me-up**
2 oz NingXia Red + 1 squirt of YL Vitality Drops - Energy Spearmint Tangerine in a glass of ice and filtered water

**05 immunity shot**
A shot of NingXia + 1 drop Thieves Vitality or Cinnamon Bark Vitality

**06 zyng bomb**
2 oz NingXia Red + 1 can of NingXia Zyng® over ice for a natural energy boost

---

So you're ready to fancy up your water or ditch the sugary soda or energy drink habit? Drinking lots of clean water is so important for the body, and sprucing it up with some of these water staples is a great way to create a new health ritual in your home. No artificial flavors, colors, sweeteners, or preservatives in the water drops (Vitality Drops) or energy drink (Zyng). They're fan favorites around here.

## *fancy up your* water habit

*citrus oils*

**CHECKLIST**

- Lemon Vitality
- Lime Vitality
- Orange Vitality
- Citrus Fresh Vitality

- NingXia Red (antioxidant drink) *must-have*
- Vitality drops (electrolyte + energy water drops)
- NingXia Zyng (natural caffeine energy drink)
- NingXia Nitro® (natural energy shot)

TARGETED SUPPORT: *energy & whole body wellness*

CHAPTER
03

# the clean home

## did you know?

Many of us unknowingly wear hundreds of toxic chemicals every day. It only takes seconds for chemicals from personal care products to get into the bloodstream. We spray air fresheners and burn candles to make our homes smell good. We use soap, lotion, sunscreen, toothpaste, perfumes, deodorant, bug spray, detergent, and household cleaners daily without knowing that many of the ingredients in these products are toxic and have never been tested for safety. But there's a better way.

## a little background

In 1976, the Toxic Substance Control Act grandfathered in thousands of chemicals that were never tested and classified them as safe. The European Union has banned over 1,328 chemicals, while the US has only banned 30. Many of the products on the store shelves contain known carcinogenic ingredients, neurotoxins, endocrine disruptors, and allergens that can be hazardous to our health. A lot of product labels have been "green-washed" to make you think they're natural when they actually aren't. Using these over a long period of time can put a toxic burden on our bodies.

## gatekeepers of our homes

We are the gatekeepers of our homes. We decide what comes into them. It's time to start educating ourselves about what's really lurking in our cabinets and begin to detox our homes, one step at a time.

Young Living® is a total wellness company that offers natural options to just about anything you could find on store shelves. When you know better, you want to do better. You and your family are worth clean, safe products, and Young Living has made it so simple to switch out any problem areas in your home that may impact yours and your family's wellbeing.

# top *ingredients* to avoid

Fragrance    Formaldehyde
"Parfum"    Propylene Glycol
Parabens    Triclosan
Phthalates    Artificial dyes
Bleach    Sulfates
Mineral Oil    Petroleum

## READ THOSE LABELS

It's so important to read those labels. Avoid using products that contain terms like "fragrance" or "parfum," as they're considered a "trade secret." Companies do not have to list those ingredients on the label. An easy way to avoid synthetic fragrances is to switch to Young Living's products that are infused with pure essential oils. They make it their mission to use the best ingredients in all of their products.

## *simple swaps* thieves line

You know that powerhouse oil we mentioned earlier called Thieves? That oil is so effective that an entire line of natural products was created using that blend. You can rest easy knowing your surfaces will actually get clean using ingredients from sweet Mother Nature. Ditch and switch products in your cabinets with harsh ingredients and swap them out for this amazing line of Thieves products. We seriously love them all.

# TOP 10

## the clean home
*simple swap guide*

**CHECKLIST** — *start here*

- Thieves® Household Cleaner
- Thieves Hand Sanitizer
- Thieves Laundry Soap
- Thieves Spray
- Thieves toothpastes & mouthwash
- Thieves Foaming Soap
- Lushious Lemon Foaming Soap
- Thieves Fruit & Veggie Soak
- Thieves Dish Soap

## ditch harsh chemicals
*one step at a time*

Search Thieves under Shop for lots more options

# THIEVES®
## all purpose cleaner

In a 16 oz glass spray bottle, add:

+ 1-2 capfuls Thieves Household Cleaner
+ 2-3 cups water

TO USE: *Give it a shake and clean. all. the. things. Ditch your other cleaners for this goodness. No harsh ingredients, plant-based, and safe for the whole family.*

CLEAN HOME
*a wellness lifestyle*

*clean home:* THIEVES

ONE BOTTLE OF
# thieves®
# household
*cleaner*
MAKES 30 SPRAY BOTTLES OF CLEANER

with 2 capfuls of Thieves Cleaner
or 60 cleaners with 1 capful

COST $23.50

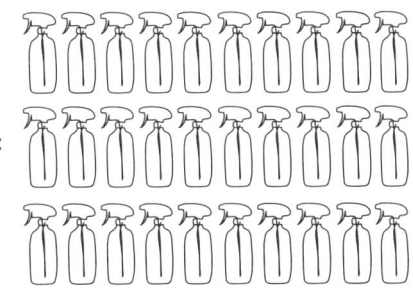

78¢ per bottle of Cleaner
*with 2 capfuls of Thieves Household Cleaner*

39¢ for 1 bottle of Cleaner *with 1 capful of Thieves Household Cleaner*

*Translation:* this one bottle of cleaner is going to last a real long time!

---

BUDGET-FRIENDLY *natural* CLEANING

At first glance, this may look like a really expensive bottle of cleaner. Oh, no, friend. This is a cleaner concentrate! A little goes a LONG way. For cents, you'll be able to mix up a 16 oz bottle of clean, plant-based cleaner, free of all the junk you'll find in most products on store shelves.

---

## *thieves cleaner*

**THE PERKS**
01/ Plant-based
02/ No harsh chemicals
03/ Safe for little ones
04/ One bottle for all the things
05/ Clean without the headache
06/ Cheaper than store cleaners
07/ Doesn't leave a residue

**CLEANS** *it all*
- Counters
- Floors
- Carpet
- Mirrors
- Glass
- Toilets
- Appliances
- Showers
- Tubs
- Toys
- Stovetop
- Oven
- Stains
- Pots & Pans

**RECIPE** *soft scrub*
+ 2 capfuls Thieves Cleaner
+ 8 drops Lemon Oil
+ 1 C Baking Soda
+ Add to a jar and mix to preferred paste consistency.

**USE ON:** *stovetops, sinks, showers, tubs, and hard-to-clean surfaces.*

# laundry
*habit*

The laundry room may just be one of the worst offenders for yucky chemicals in a home. Traditional detergents and dryer sheets contain synthetic fragrances and harsh chemicals that can wreak havoc on our bodies. Our skin is our largest organ, so let's not wear this on our clothes all day, ok? Do some digging and you'll find that asthma and respiratory symptoms, skin issues, migraines, cancer, neurological issues, and more may be caused by some of those harsh chemicals. What we put IN and ON our bodies can create a toxic burden over time. That fake blue, floral-smelling, chemically laced detergent isn't worth your health.

## natural laundry tips

So what to do? Look for plant-based ingredients with no synthetic fragrances. We promise you won't miss that headache. Remember, synthetic fragrances are engineered in a lab, often using petroleum and other ingredients that aren't required to be listed on the bottle. We avoid "fragrance" as an ingredient for that reason and use real plant juice for all the smell-good vibes now—AKA the best essential oils.

If you need a natural fabric softener, try a little bit of vinegar! Save some dollar bills and ditch those dryer sheets and grab some wool dryer balls from Amazon or Etsy instead. Toss in at least 4 or 5 for a big load. To avoid static, dry on low heat and make sure not to overdry your clothes. You can add some safety pins to a couple of the wool balls for some extra static-fighting power, if you need. We love adding a few drops of our favorite oils right on the wool balls for a subtle, clean scent.

## thieves® laundry soap

Now meet our beloved Thieves Laundry Soap. It's a super concentrated, plant-based detergent infused with pure essential oils and enzymes that help to really clean those clothes well. This small bottle packs a punch, though, giving you up to 64 loads with its 32 ounces. It's an easy button for natural laundry with ingredients you don't have to fret over.

# thieves® laundry soap

*the perks*

**01/** Free from SLS, dyes, petrochemicals, formaldehyde, phosphates, synthetic perfumes, chlorine, and optical brighteners.

**02/** Safe and gentle for babies, kids, and those with the most sensitive skin.

**03/** Fights dirt, stains, and strong odors and leaves clothes with a fresh, subtle citrus scent.

### dryer balls

Ditch the toxic dryer sheets and grab some wool dryer balls instead. Add a few drops of oil to balls for a fresh scent and toss them in.

**LAUNDRY OILS:**

| | |
|---|---|
| Lavender | Eucalyptus |
| Citrus Fresh™ | Purification® |
| Lemongrass | Lemon |

*Or any of your favorite oil scents*

CLEAN HOME: *gatekeepers*

*lushious body spray*

In a 4 oz glass spray bottle, add: 25 drops Lushious Lemon oil, 1 oz Vodka, and top with distilled water. Give it a shake and spray all over everything and smell DIVINE.

## the natural home
### RECIPES

*Lavender Lemon*
**LINEN SPRAY**

In a 8 oz glass spray bottle, add ingredients and fill remainder with distilled water.

INGREDIENTS:

+ 15 drops Lavender
+ 8 drops Lemon
+ 8 drops Eucalyptus Radiata
+ 8 drops Cedarwood
+ 2 oz vodka or witch hazel
+ 4 oz distilled water

TO USE: *Shake and spritz your sheets and pillows before bedtime. Freshen up your bath, guest beds, sofa, or anywhere that needs a boost.*

*Eucalyptus Mint Daily*
**SHOWER SPRAY**

In a 16 oz glass spray bottle, add ingredients and fill remainder with distilled water.

INGREDIENTS:

+ 15 drops Peppermint
+ 15 drops Eucalyptus or Raven™
+ 2 capfuls Thieves® Cleaner
+ 8 oz Vodka (bacteria, mildew, & soap buildup)
+ Distilled water

TO USE: *Shake and spray daily after showering to prevent soap scum buildup and keep that shower fresh and clean. Smells amazing too.*

CLEAN HOME: *gatekeepers*

*clean home*

# citrus fresh™ 
*A blend of citrus oils that can uplift mood, freshen the air, and spark creativity.*

**WAYS TO USE:**
- Diffuse with Peppermint for energy and focus.
- Ditch candles and diffuse for that "clean house" scent.
- Add drops to wool dryer balls and ditch dryer sheets.
- Add drops to spray bottle with water for a room spray.
- Add a drop of Citrus Fresh Vitality™ in water to curb appetite.

**OILS IN THIS BLEND:**
*Orange + Tangerine + Grapefruit + Lemon + Mandarin + Spearmint*

# lemon 
*Happy Vibes. Cleaning & Cleansing.*

**WAYS TO USE:**
- Remove crayon, sticky residue, or tough stains with a drop of Lemon.
- Diffuse for all the happy vibes and mood-boosting benefits.
- Add a drop of Lemon Vitality in water in the mornings to support cleansing and normal digestion. This oil loves your kidneys, bladder, and liver. It's high in limonene, a powerful antioxidant. Lemon Vitality supports a happy immune system too!

*on the go essentials*

**01 MINI THIEVES SPRAY**
The cleaning power of Thieves® oil in a tiny bottle. Toss in purse and spray on shopping cart handles, tables, in public bathrooms or dirty places on the go. Skip those popular chemical-laden wipes and use this instead.

**02 THIEVES HAND SANITIZER**
Our go-to for killing 99.99% of germs when out and about. Free of nasty ingredients and infused with aloe, Thieves, and Peppermint essential oils. Plus, this stuff won't dry your hands out.

**03 GRAPEFRUIT LIP BALM**
Makes lips soft like butter. You won't be able to go back to the store bought-stuff. Super cheap too, this will be a great one to add to your Subscribe Order.

CLEAN HOME: *gatekeepers*

# *ditch candles + diffuse*
# diffuser blends

# fresh & clean *diffuser blends*

## clean house
+ 3 Lemon
+ 3 Citrus Fresh™
+ 3 Stress Away™

## candle dupe
+ 5 Valor®
+ 5 Christmas Spirit™

## creamsicle
+ 4 Orange
+ 4 Vanilla

## anthro
+ 4 Grapefruit
+ 4 Orange
+ 2 Geranium
+ 2 Idaho Blue Spruce
+ 2 Lime

## peachy
+ 3 Valor
+ 3 Cedarwood
+ 3 Orange

## focus
+ 3 Lime
+ 2 Cedarwood
+ 2 Peppermint

## lemon bars
+ 2 Lemon
+ 2 Vanilla
+ 2 Cinnamon Bark
+ 2 Lemon Myrtle

## spring day
+ 3 Lemon
+ 3 Lavender
+ 3 Peppermint

## house guest
+ 3 Lime
+ 3 Orange
+ 2 Peppermint

## pink lemonade
+ 5 Lemon
+ 5 Valor

## lush lemon
+ 2 Lemon
+ 2 Lemon Myrtle
+ 2 Ylang Ylang
+ 2 Eucalyptus Globulus
+ 1 Cinnamon Bark
(or Lushious Lemon oil)

## sunshine
+ 3 Grapefruit
+ 2 Cedarwood
+ 3 Lime

## limeade
+ 6 Lime
+ 1 Basil
+ 2 Spearmint
+ 2 Stress Away

## SWEATER WEATHER
*diffuser blend*

+ 4 Christmas Spirit™
+ 4 Orange

# cozy diffuser blends

## pumpkin spice
+ 4 Orange
+ 3 Cinnamon
+ 2 Clove
+ 1 Nutmeg

## cozy flannel
+ 5 Bergamot
+ 4 Orange
+ 3 Stress Away™

## cider & donuts
+ 2 Orange
+ 3 Cinnamon Bark
+ 3 Stress Away
+ 1 Nutmeg

## autumn anthro
+ 4 Grapefruit
+ 3 Christmas Spirit™
+ 3 Bergamot
+ 2 Clove

## log cabin
+ 2 Eucalyptus Radiata
+ 2 Cinnamon Bark
+ 2 Northern Lights Black Spruce
+ 4 Orange

## chai latte
+ 3 Clove
+ 1 Black Pepper
+ 2 Cardamom
+ 1 Cassia
+ 2 Cinnamon Bark
+ 1 Ginger

## fireside
+ 3 Cinnamon Bark
+ 3 Northern Lights Black Spruce
+ 3 Orange

## marshmallow pumpkin spice
+ 4 Nutmeg
+ 4 Cinnamon Bark
+ 4 Ylang Ylang
+ 2 Bergamot
+ 2 Stress Away™

## apple pie
4 drops Cinnamon Bark
2 drops Lemongrass
2 Grapefruit
2 Bergamot

## hippie christmas
+ 6 Christmas Spirit
+ 2 Patchouli

## mulled cider
+ 4 Tangerine
+ 4 Bergamot
+ 3 Clove
+ 3 Cinnamon Bark
+ 3 Lemon

## fall sangria
+ 4 Lime
+ 4 Grapefruit
+ 4 Cinnamon Bark
+ 2 Copaiba

## *how to make a* DIFFUSER BOMB

Have a go-to diffuser recipe that you're constantly throwing in? Mix up a diffuser bomb for quick and easy diffusing. Grab a 1 or 2 oz dropper bottle and oils from your favorite diffuser recipe. Multiply recipe x 10 or more, depending on bottle size. Gently swirl to mix. When you're ready to diffuse, add 6-8 drops to diffuser.

# bedroom diffuser blends

## calm
+ 3 Lavender
+ 3 Stress Away™
+ 3 Frankincense

## goodnight
+ 4 Lavender
+ 4 Peace & Calming

## sleep bomb
+ 2 Cedarwood
+ 2 Peace & Calming
+ 2 Lavender

## tranquil
+ 3 Lavender
+ 3 Cedarwood
+ 3 Roman Chamomile

## floral woods
+ 3 Lavender
+ 3 Ylang Ylang
+ 4 Pine

## date night
+ 3 Idaho Blue Spruce
+ 3 Ylang Ylang
+ 3 Orange

## campout
+ 4 Grapefruit
+ 4 Northern Lights Black Spruce

## fresh linen
+ 3 Eucalyptus
+ 2 Lavender
+ 2 Lemon
+ 2 Tea Tree
+ 1 Peppermint

## winter romance
+ 6 Christmas Spirit™
+ 3 Ylang Ylang

## let it go
+ 4 Release
+ 4 Peppermint

## cozy blanket
+ 5 Northern Lights Black Spruce
+ 3 Stress Away
+ 2 Cedarwood
+ 2 Lavender
+ 2 Clove

## good vibes
+ 3 White Angelica™
+ 5 Orange
+ 3 Pine

## lullaby
+ 4 SleepyIze
+ 2 Tangerine

**CANDLE SWAP** *Did you know that burning scented candles can release volatile organic compounds (VOCs) that may increase your cancer risk? Ditch those toxic candles and diffuse instead.*

DIFFUSER BLENDS: *bedroom*

## wellness diffuser blends

### sniffles
+ 3 Raven™
+ 2 Thieves
+ 2 Lavender

### wellness
+ 3 Thieves®
+ 3 Lemon
+ 3 Peppermint

### unwind
+ 3 Lavender
+ 3 Stress Away™

### seasonal woes
+ 3 Lemon
+ 3 Lavender
+ 3 Peppermint

### breathe easy
+ 3 Lemon
+ 3 Raven
+ 2 Frankincense

### stressed out
+ 3 Frankincense
+ 3 Lavender
+ 3 Stress Away

CHAPTER
04

# oily life
*daily routines*

*oils all day*

FOR HER, FOR HIM, FOR LITTLES
*from morning until evening*

## *glowy, beautiful skin*
# self-care

Over 1,300 toxic chemicals are banned from use in Europe, but the USA only bans 30. The USA is highly unregulated and harmful ingredients are permitted in our skincare and makeup products. Many of these chemicals are linked to cancer, endocrine disruption, reproductive toxicity, organ toxicity, neurotoxicity, and many other health concerns.

## *first steps to natural skincare*

01/ Support a smooth complexion and aging skin by adding a drop of Frankincense to your facial moisturizer every night.

02/ Add a drop of Lemon to oily skin or blemishes.

03/ Mix up a facial serum with Lavender and Frankincense.

04/ Drop Lavender topically onto skin irritations.

05/ Apply Tea Tree oil topically to blemishes.

*daily routines:* SKIN

*recipe*

## GLOWY SKIN SERUM

In a glass dropper bottle, add EO's and carrier oil and gently swirl to mix.

**INGREDIENTS:**

+ 10 drops Lavender
+ 10 drops Frankincense
+ Grapeseed or Jojoba Oil

**OPTIONAL BUT DREAMY OILS TO ADD:**
*3 drops Blue Tansy & 8 droppers of Rose CBD Beauty Boost*

**TO USE:** *Apply to face at night after cleansing for glowy skin.*

*beauty swaps*

A few natural beauty favorites free of harsh ingredients and infused with pure goodness.

**SKIN FAVORITES:**

BLOOM Skincare Line *(brightening)*
CBD Beauty Boost *(lovely)*
Savvy Minerals Makeup line
Young Living lip balms
Mirah® Cleansing Oil *(dreamy)*
ART® Intensive Moisturizer
Orange Blossom Charcoal Bar

# stress away
™*Uplift & Chill out. Vacation in a bottle. Combats normal everyday stresses. Can help induce relaxation.*

**WAYS TO USE:**
- Apply to neck or wrists to calm and enjoy the aroma.
- Add a few drops to an epsom salt bath in the evening.
- Replace chemical-laden perfumes with Stress Away.

**OILS IN THIS BLEND:**
*Copaiba + Lime + Cedarwood + Vanilla + Ocotea + Lavender*

**SIMPLE SWAP:** *natural* **PERFUME**

Did you know perfumes at the store are full of fragrance, which is a known endocrine disruptor with links to cancer & infertility? Yuck! Toss that in the trash, sis!

Simple Swap: Ditch the chemical perfumes for a natural perfume roller. Roll on Stress Away on wrists as your own natural perfume that comes with the calming benefits of Stress Away oil.

## *natural* PERFUME ROLLER RECIPES
In a 10 ml glass roller, add oils + carrier oil

**HAPPY DAY** *10 drops Valor®, 10 drops Joy™, 10 drops Frankincense*

**STRESS** *10 drops Stress Away, 10 drops Joy, 10 drops Orange*

**UNICORN** *10 drops Joy, 5 drops Release™, 5 drops SARA™, 5 drops Bergamot, 10 drops Grapefruit*

**DATE NIGHT** *10 drops Sensation™, 10 drops Orange, 5 drops Idaho Blue Spruce*

SELF CARE: *natural perfume*

# self-care
*daily mood and hormone routine* for her

**01/** 2+ drops of Progessence Plus™ applied to forearms mornings or evenings for happy progesterone levels.

**02/** Endoflex™ oil applied over thyroid or adrenals for healthy energy levels and endocrine system support.

**03/** A drop of Joy™ or Valor® over heart in the mornings to uplift mood.

**04/** Support body with clean supplements. Master Formula™ and FemiGen are favorites for supporting hormones and healthy libido levels.

**05/** Clary Sage or Sclaressence™ on ankles or vitality versions in capsules for natural estrogen support.

## oils & intimacy

*in the mood*

**SENSATION** Apply Sensation™ oil to inner thighs. Use Sensation Massage oil as a natural lubricant.

*inner thigh potion*

In a 10 ml roller, add:
+ 10 drops Sensation
+ 10 drops Orange
+ 10 drops Cypress
+ Sensation Massage Oil as carrier

MADE FOR LIVING

ABODE

# for him
*daily mood and hormone routine*

01/ Ditch the cologne. Apply Shutran™ to forearms in mornings for mood and hormone support.

02/ Apply Mister™ to inner and outer ankles. Can be used along with Prostate Health™ supplement.

03/ Add a drop of Valor® to wrists to aproach the day with courage and confidence.

04/ Support body with clean supplements. Master Formula™ and PowerGize™ are favorites for men.

05/ Ditch the toxic fragranced soaps and shower with Shutran or Valor bar soap.

---

*recipe*

### MANLY MAN GOOD MOOD ROLLER

In a 10 ml roller, add essentials oils and top with carrier oil

OILS:
+ 18 drops Shutran
+ 12 drops Orange
+ 10 drops Cedarwood
+ carrier oil of choice

TO USE: *Roll on forearms and wrists in the morning.*

---

*diffuser blends for him*

### man cave
+ 3 Black Spruce
+ 3 Valor
+ 1 Wintergreen
+ 3 Bergamot

### nature hike
+ 3 Bergamot
+ 3 Cedarwood
+ 3 Orange

### office day
+ 6 Lime
+ 2 Eucalyptus Radiata
+ 4 Cedarwood

YOUNG LIVING
Thieves
Fresh Essence Plus
MOUTHWASH
Essential Oil-Infused
8 fl. oz. [236 ml]
YOUNG LIVING
Essential Oil-Infused
WHITENING
Toothpaste
Thieves
AROMABRIGHT
Thieves

*clean up your cabinets*

# simple swaps

When you're ready to level up your personal care routine, you'll find everything you need right here. We are SO much more than essential oils. From toothpaste to makeup, shampoo, lotion, skincare, and body wash—Young Living® is our favorite one-stop shop.

## 01 — *natural* DENTAL CARE
- *thieves & kidscents toothpastes -*

## 02 — *clean* MAKEUP
- *savvy minerals -*

## 03 — *natural* SKIN &
- *personal care products -*

Our signature Thieves® lines is the perfect natural solution to fresh, clean dental care. Dental care shouldn't have to come with warning labels. You won't find fluoride or any synthetics in our toothpaste and mouthwash. Our ingredients are far superior. It'll even make your dentist jealous.

Let's clean up that makeup bag. Say hello to Savvy Minerals, the new standard in clean beauty. The best thing you could put on your skin. Free of cheap fillers, synthetics, and 2,500 questionable ingredients and filled with nothing but pure goodness.

There's no need to fight acne or wrinkles with harsh chemicals. We provide natural solutions for every age, making it easy to fall in love with natural skin care & personal care. When you're ready to level up your routines, we think you'll find everything you need here.

## *favorite bathroom swaps*

| | | |
|---|---|---|
| Thieves Aromabright Toothpaste | Savvy Minerals Lipgloss | Lavender Mint Conditioner |
| Thieves Whitening Toothpaste | Savvy Minerals Foundation | Peppermint Cedarwood Bar Soap |
| Thieves Floss | Savvy Minerals Eye palettes | Valor Bar Soap |
| Thieves Mouthwash | Poppy Seed Lip Scrub | Mirah® Lustrous Hair Oil |
| Kidscents® Toothpaste | Coconut-Lime Body Butter | Lushious Lemon Lotion |

# oily routines for littles

# daily routines

There's a whole line of clean, plant-based products and oils called KidScents®. The oils are pre-diluted and ready to apply when a need pops up. Super easy for busy mamas and papas. Don't forget to try the kids' vitamins, probiotics, and toothpaste too. They'll be household staples in no time and safer than anything you'd find on store shelves.

## sniffleease™ *respiratory support*

**WAYS TO USE:**
- A Fall and Winter must-have oil for little ones.
- Apply to chest or bottoms of feet when needed.
- Diffuse with Lavender at bedtime.

## owie™ *bandaid in a bottle*

**WAYS TO USE:**
- Perfect oil to have in your arsenal for accidents.
- Apply to skin before adding a bandaid.

## tummygize™ *tummy trouble relief*

**WAYS TO USE:**
- Roll around belly button and on stomach when feeling uneasy.

## sleepyize™ *dreamy sleep*

**WAYS TO USE:**
- Apply to bottoms of feet or wrists for naps and bedtime.
- Diffuse with Tangerine for peaceful sleep.

## geneyus™ *focus and concentration in a bottle*

**WAYS TO USE:**
- Apply to back of neck before school or during homework time.
- Diffuse for focus and concentration.

## kidpower™ *calming and courage*

**WAYS TO USE:**
- The kid calmer. Apply for big feelings of worry and fear.
- Apply to wrists for the before-school butterflies.

DAILY ROUTINES: *for littles*

## DAILY IMMUNE ROLLER *recipe*

In a 10 ml roller, add essentials oils and top with carrier oil

**OILS:**
+ 10 drops Thieves®
+ 5 drops Frankincense
+ 5 drops Lemon

**TO USE:** *Our go-to roller blend in the Winter months. Roll on feet or spine before school or work.*

## *tips before heading to school*

**01/ WELLNESS** Apply Thieves roller on feet and down spine for immunity boost. Drink 1 ounce NingXia Red® before school for total body wellness.

**02/ FOCUS** Apply Geneyus™ on back of neck for focus. Diffuse Cedarwood + Lime + Peppermint in afternoons during homework time.

**03/ EMOTIONS** Apply KidPower™ on wrists for courage and confidence. Apply Peace & Calming to help calm big emotions.

**04/ NUTRITION** Take MightyVites™ —a full range of vitamins, minerals, antioxidants, and phytonutrients that deliver whole-food multinutrient support to your child's general health and well-being.

DAILY ROUTINES: *for littles*

# bedtime routine
## for littles

**daily routines**

### 01 SLEEPY TIME RUB

Set the tone for bedtime with a calming back massage or foot rub, infused with oils known to help with sleep. In a 4 oz jar, add:

INGREDIENTS:
+ 10 drops Lavender
+ 10 drops Frankincense
+ 1/2 C Coconut Oil
+ 10 drops Peace & Calming®
+ 10 drops Cedarwood

Mix all ingredients together in your glass jar and apply to bottoms of feet.

### 02 nighty night diffuser blends

Fill up diffusers in the evenings to set the stage for a good night of sleep for littles.

**LULLABY**
+ 3 SleepyIze™
+ 3 Tangerine

**HAPPY**
+ 3 Tangerine
+ 3 KidPower™

**SNIFFLES**
+ 3 SniffleEase™
+ 3 Lavender

**SWEET DREAMS**
+ 6 Seedlings Calm

**CALMING**
+ 2 Lavender
+ 3 Peace & Calming

**WELLNESS**
+ 3 Frankincense
+ 3 Lavender

### 03 sleep tight PILLOW SPRAY

+ 10 Lavender
+ 10 Roman Chamomile
+ 10 Orange

Add oils to to 4 oz spray bottle with a splash of witch hazel or vodka. Fill remainder with distilled water. Give it a shake and spritz pillows, blankets, or lovies before bed.

### 04 TANTRUM TAMER

Apply Endoflex™ over liver and White Angelica℠ on tops of shoulders when dealing with intense emotions in little ones.

### 05 MIGHTYPRO™

A blend of prebiotics and probiotics to support digestive and immune health. Take at bedtime before brushing with Kidscents® toothpaste. Tastes like a pixie stick!

DAILY ROUTINES: *for littles*

# dilution guide
## *for kids and babies*

Add essential oils to 10 ml roller bottle and top with carrier oil of choice. The bottoms of the feet are a perfect place to apply oils to the littlest ones. Keep in mind when mixing roller recipes that there's no perfect recipe or amount of drops. Have fun with it! These are just suggestions to help guide you as you get started.

### DILUTION SUGGESTIONS

*diluted in 10 ml carrier oil*

| NEWBORN | 2-6 MOS. | 6-12 MOS. | 1-4 YRS. |
|---|---|---|---|
| 1 drop | 1-2 drops | 3 drops | 4-8 drops |

## *for* babies

Oh, baby! We're in love with all things Seedlings® these days. With clean ingredients and pure oils, you never have to worry about what's going on your little one's skin. From diaper rash cream to shampoo and baby oil, they've got you covered without ever leaving your home. Way to hit the easy button on parenting.

## baby & kid *swaps*

- Baby Wipes: Seedlings Baby Wipes
- Seedlings wash
- Seedlings Calm essential oil
- Seedlings Baby Oil
- Seedlings Linen Spray
- Diaper rash cream
- KidScents® toothpaste (no flouride!)
- Kidscents shampoo & body wash
- Rose Ointment™ (for skin iritations)

DAILY ROUTINES: *for littles*

*oily tip*

### HAPPY GUMS

Apply a drop of Copaiba Vitality™ onto finger and rub on baby's gums to soothe when the need arises.

---

*recipe*

### EAR ROLLER

In a 10 ml roller, add essential oils and top with carrier oil

OILS:
+ 5 drops Melrose™
+ 5 drops Lavender

TO USE: *roll around ears (not inside) and down eustachian tubes on sides of neck. Use along with Wellness Roller (pg 17).*

---

*oily tip*

### CLEAR SKIN

Mix a drop of Lavender and Gentle Baby™ essential oils with a dollop of Rose Ointment™ or Coconut Oil and rub onto areas on skin that need to be soothed.

DAILY ROUTINES: *for littles*

## LIQUID CALM ROLLER *recipe*

In a 10 ml roller, add essentials oils and top with carrier oil

OILS:

+ 40 drops Lavender
+ 25 drops Stress Away™
+ 30 drops Valor®
+ 10 drops Patchouli
+ 12 drops Vetiver
+ top with carrier oil or CBD Oil Base

TO USE: *When you really need to calm the heck down, you'll want to whip out this amazing roller. Roll it on wrists, chest, around ears, and relax. Smells incredible too.*

*oils and emotions*

# oils & emotions

Chronic stress can really take a toll on our bodies and lead to all kinds of health problems. But thank goodness we've got our oils, as they can have a powerful effect on our emotions.

Emotions can be stored at a cellular level in specific organs within the body and they must be cleared at this level in order to be released. Essential oils access these stuck emotions at their deepest levels by accessing the limbic portion of the brain, which is the seat of emotions. Essential oils work holistically, addressing the body in all of its capacities: spiritual, emotional, mental, and physical.

*emotions stored in the body*

A lot of the physical things we deal with day to day have roots in emotion…or what we more commonly refer to as stress. Medical science has said for a long time that anger affects our liver, we can store stress and tension in our neck, anxiety in our stomach, happiness and grief in our heart, and so on. Let's work on some simple ways we can use this powerful plant juice to support emotions.

*healthy emotions*

01/ Add a drop of Valor® to your wrists in the morning to boost emotions and face the day with courage and confidence.

02/ Feeling a little frazzled? Need to calm kiddos down? Grab Peace & Calming®. Apply to wrists and back of neck.

03/ Add a drop of Stress Away™, Lavender, and Frankincense to palms, cup over nose and take deep breaths when feeling anxious.

04/ Apply a couple drops of Stress Away to wrists or behind ears for a calming effect (and to smell amazing!)

*oils and emotions*

## valor®
*One of the best oils for emotional support. This is a go-to for bravery, confidence, and all the feels.*

**WAYS TO USE:**
- Apply on wrists each morning to face the day with confidence.
- Our bravery and "I can do hard things" oil.
- Apply before the big game, test, presentation, or challenge.
- Inhale and apply over heart when emotions are running high.
- Candle dupe: Diffuse 3 drops Valor, 3 drops Christmas Spirit™

**OILS IN THIS BLEND:**
*Black Spruce + Blue Tansy + Frankincense + Geranium*

## peace & calming®
*Calm the Crazy. Rest and relax.*

**WAYS TO USE:**
- Apply to wrists to calm when nerves are rattled.
- A bedtime favorite. Apply to bottoms of feet for sweet sleep.

**OILS IN THIS BLEND:**
*Tangerine + Orange + Patchouli + Ylang Ylang + Blue Tansy*

---

**LET IT GO**
*diffuser blend*

+ 4 Release™
+ 4 Peppermint

---

*emotions guide*

- **ANGER** *Let it go and apply Release over liver.*
- **GRIEF & SADNESS** *Apply Joy™ over heart to uplift emotions.*
- **NEGATIVITY & WORRY** *Apply White Angelica™ on tops of shoulders.*
- **ABUSE** *Diffuse SARA™ to help release past trauma.*
- **STRESS** *Roll Stress Away™ on wrists, around ears, and back of neck.*

ALL THE FEELS

# bedtime
*oily routines*

# bedtime
*wind down routine*

**01/** Wind down in the evening—add Lavender and Peace & Calming® to your diffuser.

**02/** Soak in a warm Epsom salt bath with a few drops of Stress Away™.

**03/** Roll Tranquil™ or CBD Calm Roll-On on wrists and chest before bed for a restful night of sleep.

## lavender
*One of the most versatile oils. Known for its calming benefits and sleepy-time vibes.*

**WAYS TO USE:**
- Diffuse with Stress Away while you drift off to sleep.
- Your skin's best friend. Apply topically to irritations.
- Rub on chest to aid with seasonal discomfort.
- Add to a spray bottle with water for a relaxing linen spray.

*If you're needing some extra help in the sleep department, try a few of these natural options and see if they help. Everyone's is different, so it may take a little trial and error to find your winners.*

## bedtime *staples*

**BEDTIME DIFFUSER FAVORITES**
- Lavender
- Cedarwood
- Roman Chamomile
- Peace & Caming
- Pine
- Black Spruce
- Tangerine
- Dream Catcher™

**BEDTIME ROLLERS**
- Tranquil™ Roll On
- Calm CBD Roll On
- Vetiver *(roll on back of neck for racing thoughts)*

### *supplements*
- SleepEssence™ *(contains melatonin)*
- Life 9® Probiotic *(gut & immune health)*
- ImmuPro™ *(contains melatonin)*

## CBD OIL

Looking for high quality CBD you can trust? We got you. Nature's Ultra CBD contains 0.0% THC and is infused with the best essential oils ever. We're big fans of the Beauty Boost for our nighttime skincare ritual and the CBD Muscle Rub when battling all that neck tension at the end of the day.

### calm cbd roll-on

The most dreamy CBD roller infused with oils known to help calm nerves and rest well at night. Apply to wrists and chest as much as you need throughout the day.

#### WHAT'S IN THIS ROLLER?

Oils: *Eucalyptus + Frankincense + Lavender + Orange + Vetiver + Ylang Ylang*

Carrier oil blend: *CBD, Apricot kernel oil, Argan oil, Avocado oil, Camellia seed oil, Evening primrose oil, Hemp seed oil, Neem oil, Rosehip seed oil, Sweet almond oil*

CHAPTER
## 05

# subscribe to save

### WHAT IS SUBSCRIBE TO SAVE?

It's only the best monthly wellness box ever. Subscribe to Save is the simplest and most cost-effective way to swap out your products with more natural options and gradually build that oil stash. Start with one area of your home and, each month, grab a few new things. Little by little, your home and your health will begin to transform with each baby step.

*how it works*

This is our monthly subscription & loyalty program. Earn points every month month to spend like a gift card. You select which items come in each box.
Free to join.  Free to cancel.

# q&a *monthly wellness box*

## What is Subscribe to Save?
It's our favorite monthly autoship order. Completely customizable to what your family needs each month. Get the best bang for your buck by ordering your oils, supplements, soap, detergent, face wash, cleaner, and NingXia Red. This is our loyalty program and it's full of rewards.

## Do I have to order the same thing each month?
No! You can customize your order each month and select frequency of subscribed items.

## Is it free?
Yes! It's free to join. Free to cancel.

### EARN LOYALTY REWARDS

| MONTHS 1-3 | MONTHS 4-24 | MONTHS 25+ |
|---|---|---|
| **10% back** | **20% back** | **25% back** |

Earn points/dollars back with each consecutive monthly Subscribe order of at least 50+ PV that you can redeem on free oils and products like a gift card.

## *the perks* — subscribe *to* save

**01/** 24% off all purchases

**02/** Free shipping on orders over 100 pv

**03/** Earn up to 25% back in points that can be spent like store credit

**04/** Receive free gifts with purchase each month at different tiers

## Is there a minimum dollar amount required for my order?

No, there is not a minimum dollar amount required for your Subscribe to Save order; however, 50+ PV each month on subscription earns you reward points (aka free stuff)!

*For more FAQs, visit our website*

# safety tips
*oily life*

## 01/white labels
*Same oil. Different Label.*

Regular labels show topical/aromatic use while the white labels show that an oil is part of the Vitality™ line. This means that the oil is FDA approved for dietary use and generally regarded as safe to ingest. Two different labels, but the exact same oil in both bottles.

## 02/oils in water

We love adding a drop or two of Vitality oil to our water or tea. Be sure to use glass or stainless steel cups. Do not put oils in plastic.

## 03/oils in sunlight

Citrus oils (such as lemon) are photosensitive, so be sure to take caution when applying to skin exposed to sunshine when going outside.

## 04/start low, go slow

We suggest applying oils to feet or spot testing on forearms when first starting out. Bottoms of feet have large pores and the skin is less sensitive there. That makes it a great place to apply when starting out.

*safety tips*

## 05/hot oils

Some oils are considered "hot," which means that they're a little spicy when applied to skin. Dilute these oils. If something ever feels too warm on the skin, add more carrier oil to the top.

*Hot oils: Cinnamon, Clove, Lemongrass, Oregano, Thyme, Exodus II™, Thieves®, and Peppermint.*

## 06/storing oils

When stored properly, your oils will not expire. We love keeping our oils out where they're easy to grab—on counters, shelves, and nightstands.

*Tips: Don't leave them in direct sunlight or in your hot car. Carrier oils do have a shelf life, so, if your EOs are mixed with a carrier oil, they will eventually expire.*

## 07/sensitive areas

Avoid getting essential oils in eyes, ears, or other sensitive areas. If you happen to get oil in your eyes, don't sweat it. Avoid splashing with water. Instead, grab a wash cloth with coconut oil or other carrier oil and gently swipe it away.

## 08/oils for littles

Many oils are totally safe for the young ones, but it's important to dilute more for babies and toddlers. A little goes a long way. A great place to apply is bottoms of feet, where skin is less sensitive. *Raven™ not intended for children under 6.

# sharing
*the oily life*

## *become a young living* brand partner

You've unboxed your oils and plant-based goodness, filled that diffuser, and now you're reaping the benefits of this wellness lifestyle. So, naturally, you can't wait to share with your bestie. Young Living® has a pretty sweet referral program that we just love. It's pretty simple. Help a friend get started with Young Living using your own referral link! You'll earn commissions on their future orders.

Maybe you want to cover the cost of your beloved oils and NingXia, maybe you just want a little side hustle. Maybe you want a residual income that far exceeds your current income (with hard but fun work, of course). Either way, the opportunity is here and it's up to you. No experience is necessary to be a part of this movement toward natural wellness in every home.

Are you ready to join us?! Let's gooooo. To become a Brand Partner, you'll want to grab your Business Essentials Kit ($30 bucks) on Young Living's website. You'll receive the RISE booklet, a step-by-step guide on hitting your goals. With this kit, your account will transition from Customer to Brand Partner status, which makes you eligible to earn a paycheck. Yay!

Most of us weren't in "sales" before we started as Brand Partners. We just shared our hearts, stories, and genuine love for this wellness lifestyle. Our community is full of inspiring humans that will lock arms with you and guide you as you begin. Not sure where to start? Ask the person who helped you get started to plug you in!

### *start your young living business*

01/ Visit Youngliving.com and login.

02/ From menu select Company > Become a Brand Partner.

03/ Select your Business Essentials Kit and add to cart and check out.

04/ Start sharing! Download the Life Steps App for even more education on Young Living oils, products, and resources for your new business.

SHARE THE OILY LIFE : *become a brand partner*

*help others on their wellness journey*

View the full YL Income Disclosure at youngliving.com
Be sure to to check out the full Compensation Plan as well.

### AVERAGE ANNUAL INCOME

rank 01 STAR $248

rank 02 SENIOR STAR $1,553

rank 03 EXECUTIVE $3,829

rank 04 SILVER $16,788

rank 05 GOLD $52,664

rank 06 PLATINUM $123,118

rank 07 DIAMOND $352,346

rank 08 CROWN DIAMOND $710,553

rank 09 ROYAL CROWN DIAMOND $1,640,839

*based on the 2020 U.S. Income Disclosure Statement*

## the perks to sharing the oily life

01/ No products or inventory needed—just what you use and love for your own home. Send your referral link and help others get wellness shipped straight to their door and get paid for it.

02/ Freedom and flexibility to grow in your own way and on your own time.

03/ The ability to create a residual income for your family is the gift that keeps giving. Wellness. Purpose. Abundance.

04/ You'll get a community that feels like a family you didn't know you were missing.

## DIFFUSER
# recipe

**DROPS   OILS**

---

## DIFFUSER
# recipe

**DROPS   OILS**

---

## DIFFUSER
# recipe

**DROPS   OILS**

---

## DIFFUSER
# recipe

**DROPS   OILS**

---

## DIFFUSER
# recipe

**DROPS   OILS**

---

## DIFFUSER
# recipe

**DROPS   OILS**

---

## DIFFUSER
# recipe

**DROPS   OILS**

---

## DIFFUSER
# recipe

**DROPS   OILS**

## DIFFUSER
# recipe

DROPS   OILS

## DIFFUSER
# recipe

DROPS   OILS

## DIFFUSER
# recipe

DROPS   OILS

## DIFFUSER
# recipe

DROPS   OILS

## DIFFUSER
# recipe

DROPS   OILS

## DIFFUSER
# recipe

DROPS   OILS

## DIFFUSER
# recipe

DROPS   OILS

## DIFFUSER
# recipe

DROPS   OILS

## DIFFUSER
# recipe

**DROPS  OILS**

## DIFFUSER
# recipe

**DROPS  OILS**

## DIFFUSER
# recipe

**DROPS  OILS**

## DIFFUSER
# recipe

**DROPS  OILS**

## DIFFUSER
# recipe

**DROPS  OILS**

## DIFFUSER
# recipe

**DROPS  OILS**

## DIFFUSER
# recipe

**DROPS  OILS**

## DIFFUSER
# recipe

**DROPS  OILS**

## DIFFUSER
# recipe

DROPS  OILS

## DIFFUSER
# recipe

DROPS  OILS

## DIFFUSER
# recipe

DROPS  OILS

## DIFFUSER
# recipe

DROPS  OILS

## DIFFUSER
# recipe

DROPS  OILS

## DIFFUSER
# recipe

DROPS  OILS

## DIFFUSER
# recipe

DROPS  OILS

## DIFFUSER
# recipe

DROPS  OILS

## DIFFUSER
# recipe

DROPS  OILS

## DIFFUSER
# recipe

DROPS  OILS

## DIFFUSER
# recipe

DROPS  OILS

## DIFFUSER
# recipe

DROPS  OILS

## DIFFUSER
# recipe

DROPS  OILS

## DIFFUSER
# recipe

DROPS  OILS

## DIFFUSER
# recipe

DROPS  OILS

## DIFFUSER
# recipe

DROPS  OILS

## OILY recipe

**INGREDIENTS**

**DIRECTIONS**

## OILY recipe

**INGREDIENTS**

**DIRECTIONS**

## OILY recipe

**INGREDIENTS**

**DIRECTIONS**

## OILY recipe

**INGREDIENTS**

**DIRECTIONS**

## OILY
# recipe

**INGREDIENTS**  **DIRECTIONS**

## OILY
# recipe

**INGREDIENTS**  **DIRECTIONS**

## OILY
# recipe

**INGREDIENTS**  **DIRECTIONS**

## OILY
# recipe

**INGREDIENTS**  **DIRECTIONS**

## OILY recipe

**INGREDIENTS**

**DIRECTIONS**

## OILY recipe

**INGREDIENTS**

**DIRECTIONS**

## OILY recipe

**INGREDIENTS**

**DIRECTIONS**

## OILY recipe

**INGREDIENTS**

**DIRECTIONS**

## OILY recipe

**INGREDIENTS**

**DIRECTIONS**

## OILY recipe

**INGREDIENTS**

**DIRECTIONS**

## OILY recipe

**INGREDIENTS**

**DIRECTIONS**

## OILY recipe

**INGREDIENTS**

**DIRECTIONS**

# oily notes

DATE:

# oily notes

DATE:

DATE:

# oily notes

DATE:

# oily notes

## quick guide
## roller blends

In a 10 ml roller bottle, add essential oils + carrier oil of choice

### energy
+ 10 Peppermint
+ 10 Citrus Fresh™

### snooze
+ 10 Lavender
+ 10 Peace & Calming®

### calm
+ 10 Stress Away™
+ 10 Lavender
+ 10 Frankincense

### immune
+ 15 Thieves®
+ 5 Frankincense

### aches
+ 10 PanAway®
+ 10 Peppermint
+ 10 Copaiba

### get well
+ 15 Thieves
+ 10 Frankincense
+ 10 Lemon

### tummy
+ 10 DiGize®
+ 5 Peppermint

### wellness
+ 15 Thieves
+ 15 Melrose™
+ 15 Lemon
+ 7 Oregano
+ 7 Frankincense

### sniffles
+ 10 Lavender
+ 10 R.C.™
+ 10 Lemon

### seasonal woes
+ 15 Lavender
+ 15 Lemon
+ 15 Peppermint

### focus
+ 10 Lavender
+ 10 Vetiver
+ 10 Cedarwood

### healthy temps
+ 10 Frankincense
+ 10 Lavender
+ 3 Peppermint

### monthly cramps
+ 15 Dragon Time™
+ 15 Lavender
+ 10 Peppermint
+ 5 PanAway

### happy ears
+ 5 Melrose or Purification®
+ 5 Lavender

### mood boost
+ 10 Joy™
+ 10 Valor®
+ 5 Frankincense

## TOP 14

# summer
*staples for natural living*

**CHECKLIST**   *start here*

- Mineral Sunscreen Lotion
- LavaDerm™ After-Sun Spray
- Insect Repellant (deet free!)
- Citronella Oil (diffuse on patio)
- Diffusing oils: Orange, Lemon, Lime, Grapefruit, Lushious Lemon, Vanilla
- Coconut Lime Body Butter
- Lushious Lemon Hand Lotion
- Poppy Seed Lip Scrub
- Grapefruit Lip Balm

## ditch harsh chemicals
*one step at a time*

# oily wishlist
## MONTHLY PLANNER

MONTH:

MONTH:

MONTH:

MONTH:

OILY PLANNER: *monthly subscription wishlist*

# oily wishlist
## MONTHLY PLANNER

MONTH:

MONTH:

MONTH:

MONTH:

OILY PLANNER: *monthly subscription wishlist*

# oily wishlist
## MONTHLY PLANNER

MONTH:

MONTH:

MONTH:

MONTH:

OILY PLANNER: *monthly subscription wishlist*

# simple swaps

## ditch and switch

Here are a few product categories that we grab through Young Living® now. They make shopping clean, plant-based products super easy and convenient.

- Essential oils & roll-ons
- Personal Care products
- Makeup & Skincare
- Household Cleaner
- Laundry Detergent
- Massage Oils
- Kid Products
- Animal Care
- Vitamins & Supplements
- Sunscreen
- Bug Repellent
- Cough Drops
- Pain Relief Cream
- After Sun-Spray
- Hormone Support
- CBD
- Energy Drinks

Check out youngliving.com for more ideas or ask the friend who gave you this guide what their favorite swap would be! The best way to switch out your products is with Subscribe to Save—earn up to 25% back on every order that you place and turn around and spend your points like a gift card.

SIMPLE SWAPS: *ditch & switch categories*

# targeted *support*

These are a few of the oils and products that we love for targeted wellness & support.

## mind

**OILS**
Awaken™, Brain Power™, Cedarwood, Frankincense, GeneYus™

**SUPPLEMENTS**
MindWise™, OmegaGize™

## sleep

**OILS**
Lavender, Cedarwood, Vetiver, Tranquil™, Peace & Calming®, Dream Catcher™, SleepyIze™

**SUPPLEMENTS**
SleepEssence™, ImmuPro™

## energy

**OILS**
En-R-Gee™, EndoFlex™, Peppermint

**SUPPLEMENTS**
NingXia Red®, NingXia Nitro®, Super B™, PowerGize™

## respiratory

**OILS**
Breathe Again™, Peppermint, R.C.™, Raven™, Eucalyptus Globulus, Lemongrass, SniffleEase™, Pine

**SUPPLEMENTS**
Thieves® Cough Drops, Thieves® Chest Rub

## immunity

**OILS**
Lemon, Thieves®, Exodus II™, Oregano, Frankincense, ImmuPower™

**SUPPLEMENTS**
NingXia Red®, Inner Defense™, ImmuPro Chewables™

## digestive

**OILS**
Copaiba, DiGize™, Peppermint

**SUPPLEMENTS**
AlkaLime®, ComfortTone®, Detoxzyme®, Essentialzyme, Life 9™, Digest + Cleanse™

## muscles & joints

**OILS**
Copaiba, Cool Azul Pain Relief™, Deep Relief™, PanAway®, Wintergreen, CBD Muscle Rub

**SUPPLEMENTS**
AminoWise™, AgilEase™, PowerGize™, BLM™, Sulfurzyme®, Golden Turmeric

## stress & emotions

**OILS**
Believe™, Calm CBD Roll-On, Frankincense, Harmony™, Joy™, Peace & Calming®, Release™, SARA™, Stress Away™, Valor®, White Angelica™

*favorite:* The Feelings™ Collection

TARGETED SUPPORT: *shop by category*

# targeted *support*

These are a few of the oils and products that we love for targeted wellness & support.

## hormones

**OILS**

*women:* Clary Sage, Dragon Time™, EndoFlex™, Progessence Plus™, Lady Sclareol™, Ylang Ylang, SclarEssence™

**SUPPLEMENTS**

CortiStop®, FemiGen™, Master Formula™, Mineral Essence

*men:* Mister™, Shutran™, Idaho Blue Spruce

**SUPPLEMENTS**

PowerGize™, Prostate Health™, Master Formula™, Mineral Essence

## skin

**OILS**

Blue Tansy, Lavender, Frankincense, Elemi, Tea Tree, Geranium, Gentle Baby™, Rose, Royal Hawaiian Sandalwood

**PRODUCTS**

Rose Ointment™, Coconut Lime Body Butter, Lushious Lemon Hand Lotion, Valor Moisturizing Soap

*skincare favorites:* BLOOM® Brightening Cleanser, CBD Beauty Boost, ART® Skin Care System, ART® Renewal Serum, Sheerlumé™, Charcoal Bar Soap

## little ones

**OILS**

SniffleEase™, TummyGize™, GeneYus™, Owie™, SleepyIze™, Gentle Baby™, Seedlings® Calm™, KidPower®

**SUPPLEMENTS**

NingXia Red®, MightyVites™, MightyZyme™, MightyPro™, Unwind™

TARGETED SUPPORT: *shop by category*

*the perfect welcome gift*
FOR A NEW OILER *by* MEGAN WRIGHT

Meet the Oily Life Guide. This guide was written and designed with a purpose: to help new members get familiar with their oils and take the next steps in their wellness journey. It's a place for oilers to learn, write their favorite diffuser recipes and oil wish lists, and take notes. We hope this guide serves as a beautiful tool for Brand Partners to grow their Young Living businesses and gift to their future members, if they so choose.

*share your guides*
We'd love to see how you're using your Oily Life Guide on Instagram! Be sure to tag us in your stories or posts.

@meganwrightdesignco | @growinghealthyhomes
#oilylifeguide

Published by Growing Healthy Homes
Copyright © 2018 by Megan Wright Design Co.
ISBN: 978-1-7370846-1-7
Design & photography by Megan Wright Design Co.
Copywriter: Abby O'Leary
Editor: Seane Thomas
Interior Designer: 25:40 Love & Co

All rights reserved. No part of this book may be used or reproduced in any manner without written permission.

meganwrightdesign.com

To purchase more guides, visit:
growinghealthyhomes.com